WOODROW *Wilson*

WOODROW *Wilson*

OUR TWENTY-EIGHTH PRESIDENT

By Carol Brunelli and Ann Graham Gaines

SPIRIT
of America®

The Child's World®
Chanhassen, Minnesota

10

Woodrow Wilson

Published in the United States of America by The Child's World®
PO Box 326 • Chanhassen, MN 55317-0326 • 800-599-READ • www.childsworld.com

Acknowledgments
The Creative Spark: Mary Francis-DeMarois, Project Director; Elizabeth Sirimarco Budd, Series Editor;
Robert Court, Design and Art Direction; Janine Graham, Page Layout; Jennifer Moyers, Production

The Child's World®: Mary Berendes, Publishing Director; Red Line Editorial, Fact Research;
Cindy Klingel, Curriculum Advisor; Robert Noyed, Historical Advisor

Photos
Cover: White House Collection, courtesy White House Historical Association; Bettmann/Corbis: 28,
36; Corbis: 14; Library of Congress: 6, 11, 22, 23, 24, 29, 30, 31, 32; National Archives: 37; Courtesy
of Princeton University: 17; Woodrow Wilson Birthplace: 9, 10, 12, 19, 21; Woodrow Wilson House:
7, 13, 16, 20, 27, 34

Registration
The Child's World®, Spirit of America®, and their associated logos are the sole property and
registered trademarks of The Child's World®.

Library of Congress Cataloging-in-Publication Data
Brunelli, Carol.
    Woodrow Wilson : our twenty-eighth president / by Carol Brunelli and Ann Graham Gaines.
        p. cm.
    Includes bibliographical references (p.   ) and index.
    ISBN 1-56766-863-1 (library bound : alk. paper)
    1. Wilson, Woodrow, 1856-1924—Juvenile literature. 2. Presidents—United States—Biography—
Juvenile literature. [1. Wilson, Woodrow, 1856-1924. 2. Presidents.]   I. Gaines, Ann. II. Title.
    E767 .B8 2001
    973.91'3'092—dc21

                                        2001000409

20   29   37

Contents

Chapter ONE

The Scholar

President Woodrow Wilson was known for his intellect. Before entering politics, he was a college professor and then president of Princeton University, one of the best schools in the nation.

THOMAS WOODROW WILSON WAS BORN ON December 28, 1856, in Staunton, Virginia. He was the son of Joseph and Janet Wilson. People called him "Tommy" until his college days, when he began to use the name Woodrow. While he was still a boy, his family moved to Georgia and then to South Carolina.

Tommy grew up during a difficult time. He was four years old when the Southern states left the **Union** to form a new nation. They called it the Confederate States of America. Soon after, the **Civil War** began. Wilson's earliest memories were of seeing Union soldiers marching into his town. After a battle took place near their home, his mother volunteered to care for wounded Confederate soldiers in the army's makeshift hospital. In 1865, the war ended when the

The Wilsons moved to this home in Columbia, South Carolina, in 1870.

South became too poor and weak to fight any longer. Confederate General Robert E. Lee surrendered to Union General Ulysses S. Grant. Tommy never forgot the day he watched Lee pass through his town as a prisoner, guarded by Union soldiers.

After the war ended, the South rejoined the Union. The period known as Reconstruction began. During this time, the nation went to work rebuilding the ruined South, which was in terrible shape after the war. Many of the farms and **plantations** lay in ruins. Tommy saw great misery. Perhaps it was his early memories of war that would make him work so hard for peace later in life, when he was president of the United States.

Tommy's parents tried to make their children's lives happy in spite of the war and its aftermath. Tommy was a smart and talented boy, but he did not do very well in school. In fact, he did not learn the alphabet until he was nine years old and could not read until age 12. Although no one knows for certain, he probably suffered from a learning disability. Even though he was not a great student, Tommy had many interests. He was not very strong, however, and had health problems all of his life. Even so, he played baseball when he could. He also loved to sing and speak in public.

After graduating from high school, Tommy attended Davidson College in Charlotte, North Carolina. By this time, he had grown to almost his full height. He was a tall, thin man with piercing eyes. By nature, Tommy was an intense person who fought for his beliefs. Those who did not know him well thought he was always serious, but his friends and family knew he could sometimes be silly.

Woodrow's parents were Joseph and Janet Wilson (shown in the photograph at left). Woodrow grew up in a very religious family. His father was a Presbyterian minister, and his mother was the daughter of a minister as well.

At college, Tommy worked hard and earned excellent grades. He especially liked classes that taught him to be a better writer and public speaker. But although Tommy liked Davidson College, he was sick so often that he left after just one year and returned home.

As a young man, Wilson seemed to be rather serious, but he enjoyed laughing and joking with his family. Unfortunately, he suffered from poor health, which kept him from being as active as he would have liked. It also made it difficult for him to complete his studies.

By 1875, Tommy's health had improved. He went back to school at the College of New Jersey (which later changed its name to Princeton University). He did very well. By the time he graduated in 1879, he had decided to become a lawyer and entered the University of Virginia Law School. But once again, Tommy (now called Woodrow) became ill and returned to his parents' home.

Woodrow Wilson never returned to law school. Instead, he studied the law on his own for three years. In October of 1882, he passed his state's bar examination, a test that allowed him to work as a lawyer. He opened a law office in Atlanta, Georgia. Woodrow had worked as a lawyer for less than a year when he realized he was no longer interested in the law.

Once more, Woodrow went back to school. This time, he enrolled at Johns Hopkins University in Baltimore. He hoped to earn a doctoral degree, which is a degree given to people who complete advanced studies at a university. He set out to study

history and politics, the work of the government. To earn his degree, he had to write a long paper about American government. This paper, titled *Congressional Government: A Study in American Politics,* was well written and researched. It was even published as a book. In this paper, Woodrow criticized the American government. He said that Congress was too strong, and that the president was too weak. But by the time he became president, Woodrow

Wilson enjoyed many activities at the College of New Jersey. He is shown here, standing third from right, with the Alligator Club. This group of students ate their meals and spent their free time together.

Even after Woodrow left South Carolina to attend school, he often returned home to visit his family. Woodrow (seated at far left) is shown here with his family around the time he attended Johns Hopkins University.

Wilson had changed his mind. He realized that the president of the United States could work to make Congress see his point of view. Strong presidents often convince members of Congress to introduce and pass **bills.**

While at Johns Hopkins University, Woodrow also spent a lot of time at activities outside the classroom. He sang in a **glee club** and was a member of the **debate** team. He had less time for such things in his last year at school because he married in June of 1885. His bride was 25-year-old Ellen Louise Axson.

After Woodrow graduated, the couple moved to Pennsylvania. Woodrow became a professor at Bryn Mawr College, where he taught classes in government from 1885 to 1888. Then he accepted a new position at Wesleyan University in Connecticut. By that time, he and Ellen had two daughters and would soon have a third. At Wesleyan, Woodrow taught history. In his free time, he wrote a textbook, called *The State,* about how different governments worked. His work was highly respected, and Woodrow Wilson was making a name for himself.

Wilson was so taken by Ellen Axson that he proposed marriage the fourth time they saw each other.

WOODROW WILSON'S FIRST WIFE, ELLEN AXSON WILSON, WAS BORN IN Savannah, Georgia. Like Woodrow, her father was a Presbyterian minister. They had both grown up in the South as well. One Sunday in 1883, Woodrow saw Ellen while attending her father's church. He liked her immediately. "What a bright and pretty face," he recalled thinking. Never one to waste time, he called on Ellen's father at once, asking to be introduced to the lovely young girl.

Woodrow and Ellen became engaged later that year but delayed their wedding until 1885, when Woodrow was close to finishing his studies at Johns Hopkins University. During this time, Ellen studied painting at the Art Students League in New York City. She loved to paint but gave it up to devote herself to her husband, whom she called "the greatest man in the world." Wilson loved Ellen equally. "My love for you," he once wrote to her, "released my real personality, and I can never express it perfectly in either act or word away from you." Ellen was an excellent wife who managed the family and home perfectly. But she was also an important partner for Woodrow. She edited his writing. She also helped him improve his speeches and learn German. Ellen was always available when Woodrow needed to solve a problem. She gave him advice and encouragement. The couple is shown at left in a photograph taken while Wilson was the governor of New Jersey.

Chapter TWO

Entry to Politics

As a professor at Princeton, Wilson was respected not only as a gifted speaker but also as a great thinker. People respected his opinions about politics and government.

IN 1890, WOODROW WILSON AND HIS FAMILY moved to New Jersey when he became a professor of law and politics at his old school, the College of New Jersey. He was a good teacher. Students said he was among the university's most popular professors.

Wilson remained very busy during this time and published nine books. "I have a passion for interpreting great thoughts to the world," he once wrote. By this he meant he liked to explain important ideas to people through speaking and writing.

After 12 years of teaching at Princeton, Wilson became the university's president in 1902. He was now in charge of the university. He hired professors and decided what classes they should teach. As soon as he started this

new job, he introduced **reforms,** changes to improve the way the school was run. Wilson borrowed an idea from one of England's finest universities, Oxford. At Oxford, tutors were available to help students learn. Wilson hired tutors to work at Princeton. The students still attended classes, but they also worked one-on-one with the tutors. They could ask questions and make sure they truly understood their lessons. Wilson wanted Princeton to be one of the best universities in the country.

The College of New Jersey became Princeton University in 1896. Other presidents have studied and worked at Princeton. James Madison graduated from the school in 1771. Grover Cleveland lectured there after his two terms as president.

17

▶ Many important people attended the ceremony where Wilson became the president of Princeton University. Among these were former U.S. president Grover Cleveland, Robert T. Lincoln (son of Abraham Lincoln), African American educator Booker T. Washington, and author Mark Twain.

▶ In 1893, Wilson published a biography of George Washington. It became a best-seller.

He made sure only the best students were accepted to study there. But even though Wilson wanted only the best for Princeton, he sometimes ran into trouble because of his strong opinions. They made it difficult for him to get along with other university officials.

Wilson had always dreamed of starting a career in politics. As president of Princeton, he had become well known in New Jersey. In 1910, members of the Democratic Party, one of the nation's two major **political parties,** asked Wilson to run for governor of New Jersey. He agreed and won the election easily.

Wilson was governor for two years. He gained a reputation as a reformer, someone who tries to improve the way the government works. Governor Wilson had many successes in a short time. One thing he did was push for a law to help workers. It paid money to families of workers who were injured or killed on the job.

By 1911, he had gained the respect of Congressman William Jennings Bryan, the leader of the National Democratic Party. Thanks to Bryan's efforts, Wilson received the Democratic Party's presidential **nomination**

in 1912. Soon after, he began his **campaign.**
He had two opponents, and both had already
served as president.

The **candidate** from the Republican Party,
William Howard Taft, had been elected in
1908. He was running for reelection. Theodore
Roosevelt had been the 26th president of the
United States. Roosevelt had hoped to win the
Republican nomination. When he did not,
he and his supporters formed a third party, the
Progressive Party. Roosevelt ran for president
as their candidate.

Governor Wilson used to say that the door to his office was always open, encouraging people to come to him with their concerns. Wilson and his secretary, Joseph Tumulty, are shown here in Wilson's office at the state house.

19

Once Taft earned the Republican nomination, he did little to win the presidency. Wilson and Roosevelt were the major candidates. They were both reformers, interested in making the United States a better place to live. They disagreed on one important issue, however. Roosevelt believed in what he called "New Nationalism." He thought the government should stop businesses from growing so large and powerful that they destroyed competition from smaller businesses. Wilson talked about an idea he called "New Freedom." He did not want the government to control big businesses. Instead, he believed the government should help Americans create small businesses. Americans liked Wilson's ideas, and in November, he won the election.

President Woodrow Wilson's inauguration took place on March 4, 1913. An inauguration is the ceremony that takes place when a new president enters office. Wilson (at far right in carriage) rode to the event in a horse-drawn carriage with the outgoing president, William Howard Taft (in center of carriage).

Chapter THREE

The Reformer

After his inauguration, President Wilson set to work at once. He hoped to make changes that would improve the federal government.

As president of Princeton University and as governor of New Jersey, Wilson had become known as someone who worked for reform. This goal continued into his first **term** as president. Now he hoped to make changes that would improve the **federal** government as well.

As soon as he took office, Wilson set out to meet his goals. During the campaign, he had talked about wanting to lower tariffs. These are special **taxes** that the government places on goods brought from other countries to sell in the United States. Wilson urged Congress to pass the Underwood Act. This new law lowered tariffs, which meant Americans paid less for goods from overseas.

Wilson had to find a way to replace the money the government lost when it lowered

the tariffs. In February of 1913, the 16th **Amendment** to the **Constitution** had taken effect. This allowed the government to tax people's incomes, the money they earned from work and other sources. The government had not yet started collecting the tax, but Wilson decided it was a good way to make up the money lost from the tariffs. He convinced Congress that the tax should not be the same for everyone. People who earned more money paid higher taxes. Poor

One of the first tasks facing a new president is the selection of a cabinet—the group of people who advise the president. Wilson (seated at far left) selected a group of intelligent and important leaders for these posts.

Americans paid lower taxes. The government could use the money it collected from income tax to pay for its programs, and this would help make up the earnings lost from the lowered tariffs.

Next, Wilson worked to reform banking. He pushed Congress to pass the Federal Reserve Act of 1913. This gave the government control

Always a fan of baseball, Wilson enjoyed the presidential tradition of throwing out the first pitch of the new baseball season.

of interest rates. Interest is money that a bank charges its customers who borrow money. Wilson believed the government should have more control over the banking business. He wanted the government to decide how much interest banks could charge. This would mean that in times of crisis, the government could allow people to pay less interest on the money they borrowed. For example, if farmers lost all of their crops because of bad weather, they might have to borrow money to pay their bills. With Wilson's new law, the government could decide to charge them less interest.

During his first term in office, Wilson also worked to improve the lives of workers. He signed the Adamson Act into law. This law led to a shorter workday of eight hours for all industrial workers. Another new law made it illegal to hire young children.

At the end of Wilson's first term, Americans were talking about problems in other countries. World War I had begun in Europe in the summer of 1914. Tensions between European nations had been building for a long time. When fighting began, Austria-Hungary and Germany were on the same side. Great Britain,

France, and Russia were on the other. Woodrow Wilson did not want the United States to join in the war. As president, he worked to convince Americans that the country should remain **neutral.** Most Americans agreed with him, but some sympathized with the British and wanted to help them fight.

As Wilson faced this problem, a very sad event occurred in his personal life. His wife, Ellen, had become ill. After months of sickness, she died on August 6, 1914. The following spring, he met a widow named Edith Galt. They married later that year. He loved Edith deeply. "I have won a sweet companion who will soon make me forget the intolerable loneliness and isolation of the weary months since this terrible war began," he once wrote.

In 1916, President Wilson decided to run for another term. His campaign slogan was "He kept us out of war." Wilson understood that the United States had to prepare for war, but he also wanted it to be ready to make peace. He spoke about his idea for an international association of nations. He hoped that the League of Nations, as he planned to call it, would help keep peace in the future.

Wilson met Edith Galt seven months after his first wife had died. When he confessed his love to her after a short time, Edith worried that it was too soon for him to fall in love again. But Wilson did not agree. "Time is not measured by weeks, or months, or years," he said, "but by deep human experiences; and since her death I have lived a lifetime of loneliness and heartache."

In the election, Wilson ran against Republican Charles Evans Hughes, a Supreme Court justice. Wilson won the election. His message of peace was what Americans wanted to hear.

AMERICA FIRST

Wilson, That's All!

Wilson decided to run for reelection in 1916. Many Americans admired his leadership during his first four years as president. He easily won the election in November.

WILSON GREW UP IN THE SOUTH. Like many southerners of his day, he did not believe that black Americans should have the same rights as other American citizens. He supported the practice of segregation, the system of laws and practices that kept blacks and whites separated. In fact, Wilson ordered that black government workers be segregated from white workers.

African American leaders criticized Wilson. In November of 1914, a group led by civil rights leader William Monroe Trotter met with Wilson at the White House. They explained that African Americans were disappointed in him. They wanted him to stop segregation in the nation's capital and in its government. Unfortunately, Wilson left the meeting, and the group was asked to leave the White House.

Segregation continued to be a problem when the United States entered World War I in 1917. Nearly 400,000 African Americans served in World War I. Unfortunately, black soldiers were generally treated poorly. Few blacks received leadership positions. In the army, they served in segregated units that received the worst assignments. The navy assigned black soldiers to food service. The U.S. Marines wouldn't accept them into their ranks at all. Even so, African American soldiers fought bravely for their country, struggling not only with war, but with discrimination as well.

Chapter FOUR

A Time of War

Wilson believed that his presidency would be spent working on issues at home in the United States. But as he entered his second term, it became clear that he would have to deal with foreign problems as well.

WOODROW WILSON HAD HOPED THE UNITED States could stay out of World War I. This became impossible during his second term when a German submarine attacked a British ship, the *Lusitania,* in May of 1915. The attack killed 1,200 of the ship's passengers, including 128 Americans. Wilson asked the Germans to promise to stop attacking unarmed ships. The Germans made this promise, but they broke it in 1917.

Finally, on April 2, 1917, President Wilson asked Congress to declare war on Germany. He read them this message: "The present German submarine warfare against commerce is a warfare against mankind. It is a war against all nations …. We are accepting this challenge…. The world must be made safe for **democracy.**"

On April 6, Congress declared war. The war gave Wilson enormous power. He took charge of the United States' telegraph and telephone systems. He also launched a major shipbuilding program and started to **ration** food. He put Herbert Hoover in charge of the nation's food supplies. (Hoover later became the 31st president of the United States.) To help ration food, Hoover asked Americans to eat no meat on "Meatless Mondays." He asked them to do without bread and other baked goods on "Wheatless Wednesdays." He encouraged Americans to grow their own vegetables.

According to the U.S. Constitution, it is the responsibility of Congress to declare war. President Wilson addressed Congress on April 2, 1917, requesting that it declare war on Germany. Four days later, on April 6, the United States entered World War I.

Although women did not fight in World War I, they contributed a great deal to the war effort. They went to work when American men left their jobs to join the military. This kept U.S. businesses open. Thousands of women also joined the military, working as clerical workers or nurses, sometimes near the front lines of battle. The woman in this photograph went to work in a metal-working factory

To pay for the war, Wilson introduced another income tax. It raised nearly half of the $33 billion the American government spent on the war. The government raised more money by selling Liberty **Bonds.** Wilson also had the power to **draft** soldiers to increase the size of the military. More than 2.8 million American soldiers fought in World War I. More than 100,000 of them died.

On January 8, 1918, Wilson had an opportunity to speak to Congress about his ideas for world peace. That day, he presented his Fourteen Points speech. Each point was an item that Wilson believed must be accomplished to end the war. The final point was his plan to found a new international organization, the League of Nations. Wilson believed that this organization could create a new era of world peace. The war ended later that year when Germany **surrendered** in November. Wilson now hoped the League of Nations could become a reality.

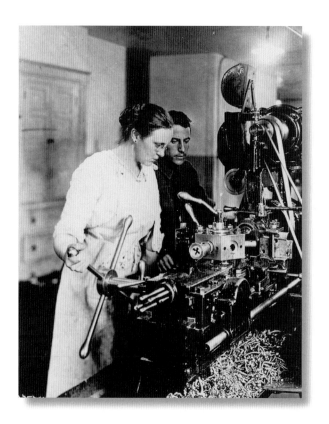

The following January, Wilson sailed to Europe to begin peace talks. He met in secret with U.S. **allies**—Great Britain, France, and Italy. Together they wrote the **Treaty** of Versailles. Among other things, it said that Germany had to pay for all of the damage caused during the war. The treaty also made plans to create the League of Nations.

When Wilson returned home, he had to convince members of the Senate to accept the Treaty of Versailles. His opponents in the Senate did not want the United States to be so involved in the League of Nations. To win support from the American people, Wilson toured the nation giving speeches. He said that U.S. leadership in the League was the only way to achieve world peace. He traveled 9,981 miles, giving speeches in 29 cities. The effort exhausted him. Still, he continued. "We cannot turn back," Wilson told Americans. "We can only go forward, with lifted eyes to follow the vision. America shall in truth show the way."

Finally, on September 25, 1919, while in Pueblo, Colorado, President Wilson collapsed. The rest of his trip was canceled, and he returned to Washington, D.C. Wilson suffered a serious **stroke** a week later. It left the left side of his body paralyzed, so he could not use one arm and one leg. After his stroke, he also found it difficult to think clearly.

Wilson still performed some of his duties as president, but he no longer appeared in public. His cabinet had to help him run the

government. When the Senate again rejected the Treaty of Versailles toward the end of Wilson's second term, he was very disappointed. "I have given my vitality, and almost my life, for the League of Nations," he said. The League was formed and held its first meeting in November, but the U.S. would never join the organization.

Wilson was not well enough to run in the presidential election of 1920. The Republican candidate, Senator Warren G. Harding, spoke about his dislike of both Woodrow Wilson and the League of Nations. He said the nation needed a "return to normalcy" after the hard times of World War I and Wilson's serious health problems. Harding easily won the election.

Wilson was rewarded for his peace efforts, however. In December of 1920, he won the Nobel Peace Prize. This important award is given once a year to the individual who has done the most to promote world peace.

Wilson's second term as president ended on March 4, 1921, when Harding entered office. Leaving the White House, Woodrow and Edith Wilson retired to a home in downtown Washington. Wilson died about three

Interesting Facts

▶ During World War I, sheep grazed on the White House lawn. They took the place of gardeners who had been drafted into the armed forces. Wilson donated the wool from the White House sheep to the Red Cross to make soldier's uniforms.

▶ During World War I, many Americans hated all things German. Phrases with the word "German" were changed. "German measles" became "liberty measles," and German shepherds were renamed "police dogs." Libraries burned German books, and schools did not teach German. Some communities even banned the music of German composers, such as Bach and Beethoven.

Interesting Facts

▸ President Franklin Roosevelt came up with the new name for the League of Nations. The name "United Nations" was first used in 1942.

▸ The United Nations headquarters is located in New York City on 16 acres of land along the East River. A wealthy businessman named John D. Rockefeller Jr. donated $8.5 million to help the organization purchase the site.

years later, on February 3, 1924. His dream of U.S. membership to the League of Nations never became a reality. The United States did join an international peacekeeping organization in future years, however. During Franklin Delano Roosevelt's presidency, the U.S. helped to found the United Nations, which replaced the League of Nations in 1946. People around the world can thank President Woodrow Wilson for the United Nations, for many of his ideas formed the basis of this organization. Its most important goal is "to save succeeding generations from the scourge of war."

Wilson's leadership resulted in the United Nations, an organization dedicated to world peace.

Beat back the HUN with LIBERTY BONDS

AT THE START OF WORLD WAR I, THE American government and its citizens worked to avoid going to war. Wilson had won reelection with the slogan, "He kept us out of war." Peace groups protested against any American involvement. But by 1917, Wilson was certain the United States had to join the fight. He needed to increase support for it among the people.

After Congress declared war in April, President Wilson created the Committee on Public Information. This group, led by a newspaper reporter named George Creel, was formed to convince Americans that going to war was the right thing to do. Creel and the committee handed out millions of pro-war pamphlets to the American people. They hung posters like the one above, depicting the enemy as a monster. Creel organized the "Four-Minute Men." These were people who gave short speeches all over the country in theaters, churches, clubs, and other public places. The speeches encouraged men to join the military, explained why the United States was fighting, and criticized the Germans. The Four-Minute Men spoke to more than 11 million people per month.

Creel and his co-workers stirred up feelings against all things German. Unfortunately, this included American citizens whose ancestors came from Germany. German Americans suffered during the war. Sometimes they were threatened or even beaten. To avoid being hurt, some Germans even changed their family names.

1856 Thomas Woodrow Wilson is born on December 28 in Staunton, Virginia.

1873 Wilson enters Davidson College in Charlotte, North Carolina.

1875 Wilson enters the College of New Jersey (which becomes Princeton University in 1896).

1879 In June, Wilson graduates from the College of New Jersey. In the fall, he enters the University of Virginia Law School.

1882 Wilson passes the Georgia bar examination, which allows him to practice law in that state. He opens an office with a friend from law school.

1883 Wilson leaves his law practice. He enrolls at Johns Hopkins University to study for a doctoral degree in history and politics. He meets his future wife, Ellen Axson.

1885 Wilson and Ellen Axson marry. He receives a doctoral degree in history and politics and then begins working as a professor of history at Bryn Mawr College.

1888 Wilson accepts a position as professor of history at Wesleyan University in Middletown, Connecticut.

1890 Wilson accepts a position as a professor of law and politics at the College of New Jersey.

1902 On October 25, Wilson becomes president of Princeton University.

1910 Wilson is elected governor of New Jersey.

1911 On January 17, Wilson becomes the governor of New Jersey. That year, Democratic Party leaders nominate him as a candidate for president of the United States.

1912 Wilson is elected the 28th president of the United States.

1913 In February, Congress and the states approve the 16th Amendment to the Constitution, which allows the federal government to collect income tax. Wilson is inaugurated on March 4. The Federal Reserve Act passes.

1914 Wilson declares that the United States will remain neutral in the war that has started in Europe. Ellen Wilson dies on August 6.

1915 On May 7, a German submarine attacks a British ship, the *Lusitania.* Wilson demands that Germany stop attacking civilian (nonmilitary) ships at sea. On December 18, he marries Edith Galt.

1916 Wilson signs an act to make child labor illegal. In November, he is reelected president of the United States.

1917 Germany resumes attacks on civilian ships. In April, Wilson asks Congress to declare war. Wilson begins new programs to ensure the United States will be victorious. More than 2.8 million men are drafted into the U.S. armed forces.

1918 On January 8, Wilson delivers his Fourteen Points speech to Congress, explaining what he believes must be accomplished to end the war. Germany accepts defeat by the Allied Powers in November.

1919 The Allies meet to define the terms of the Treaty of Versailles to end World War I. In June, the signing of the Treaty of Versailles officially ends World War I. Part of the treaty includes the creation of the League of Nations, which Wilson firmly supports. He must convince the Senate to accept the terms of the treaty. In September, Wilson suffers a stroke that leaves the left side of his body paralyzed. In November, the Senate rejects the Treaty of Versailles because senators do not support the League of Nations.

1920 The Senate rejects the Treaty of Versailles a second time. Congress declares the war over, but never agrees to all the terms of the treaty—including the League of Nations. In November, Warren G. Harding wins the presidential election. Later that month, the League of Nations holds its first meeting. The United States will never join the organization. In December, Wilson wins the Nobel Peace Prize for his efforts to bring about world peace.

1921 Wilson's second term ends when Warren G. Harding enters office. The Wilsons move into a townhome in Washington, D.C.

1924 On February 3, Thomas Woodrow Wilson dies in Washington, D.C.

1946 The League of Nations is replaced by the United Nations (UN), an international organization dedicated to world peace. The United States is among the UN's founding members.

allies (AL-lize)
Allies are nations that have agreed to help each other by fighting together against a common enemy. France, Great Britain, and Italy were U.S. allies during World War I.

amendment (uh-MEND-ment)
An amendment is a change or addition made to the U.S. Constitution or other documents. In February of 1913, Congress passed the 16th Amendment.

bills (BILZ)
Bills are ideas for new laws that are presented to a group of lawmakers. Some presidents can convince Congress to introduce and pass bills.

bonds (BONDZ)
Bonds are certificates issued by a government that promise to pay back (with interest) money borrowed from the buyer of the certificate. During World War I, the government raised money by selling Liberty Bonds.

campaign (kam-PAYN)
A campaign is the process of running for an election, including activities such as giving speeches or attending rallies. Wilson began his first campaign for president in 1912.

candidate (KAN-dih-det)
A candidate is a person running in an election. Wilson was the Democratic Party's presidential candidate in 1912 and 1916.

Civil War (SIV-il WAR)
The Civil War was a war between the northern and southern states from 1861 to 1865. Wilson was just 4 years old when the Civil War began.

constitution (kon-stih-TOO-shun)
A constitution is the set of basic principles that govern a state, country, or society. According to the U.S. Constitution, only Congress can declare war.

debate (deh-BAYT)
A debate is a formal meeting in which people discuss different opinions on a topic. While at Johns Hopkins, Wilson belonged to a a team of students who debated ideas in their free time.

democracy (deh-MOK-ruh-see)
A democracy is a nation in which the people control the government by electing their own leaders. The United States is a democracy.

draft (DRAFT)
When governments draft people into the armed forces, they require them to join. The U.S. government drafted more than 2.8 million men during World War I.

federal (FED-er-ul)
Federal means having to do with the central government of the United States, rather than a state or city government. Wilson planned to reform the federal government.

Glossary Terms

glee club (GLEE KLUB)
A glee club is a group of people who sing songs together. Wilson sang in a glee club while he was at Johns Hopkins University.

neutral (NOO-trul)
If a country is neutral, it does not take sides during a conflict or war. Wilson wanted the United States to remain neutral during World War I.

nomination (nom-ih-NAY-shun)
If someone receives a nomination, he or she is chosen by a political party to run for an office. Wilson received the Democratic Party's presidential nomination in 1912 and 1916.

plantations (plan-TAY-shunz)
Plantations are large farms or groups of farms that grow crops such as tobacco, sugarcane, or cotton. After the Civil War, many southern plantations were destroyed.

**political parties
(puh-LIT-ih-kul PAR-teez)**
Political parties are groups of people who share similar ideas about how to run a government. The two major political parties in the United States are the Democratic Party and the Republican Party.

ration (RASH-un)
If people ration something, they only distribute a small amount of it. During World War I, the U.S. government rationed food supplies.

reforms (reh-FORMZ)
Reforms are changes that improve something. As an educator and a politician, Wilson introduced reforms.

stroke (STROHK)
A stroke is a sudden injury to the brain that occurs when a blood vessel breaks or becomes blocked. Wilson suffered a stroke in 1919.

surrender (suh-REN-dur)
If an army surrenders, it gives up to its enemy. The Germans surrendered in 1918.

taxes (TAK-sez)
Taxes are payments of money made by citizens to support a government. The 16th Amendment allowed the government to collect taxes on people's incomes.

term (TERM)
A term is the length of time a politician can keep his or her position by law. A U.S. president's term of office is four years.

treaty (TREE-tee)
A treaty is a formal agreement between nations. The Treaty of Versailles ended World War I.

union (YOON-yen)
A union is the joining together of two people or groups of people, such as states. During the Civil War, the Union was another name for the United States.

Our PRESIDENTS

President	Birthplace	Life Dates	Term	Political Party	First Lady
George Washington	Virginia	1732–1799	1789–1797	None	Martha Dandridge Custis Washington
John Adams	Massachusetts	1735–1826	1797–1801	Federalist	Abigail Smith Adams
Thomas Jefferson	Virginia	1743–1826	1801–1809	Democratic-Republican	widower
James Madison	Virginia	1751–1836	1809–1817	Democratic-Republican	Dolley Payne Todd Madison
James Monroe	Virginia	1758–1831	1817–1825	Democratic-Republican	Elizabeth "Eliza" Kortright Monroe
John Quincy Adams	Massachusetts	1767–1848	1825–1829	Democratic-Republican	Louisa Catherine Johnson Adams
Andrew Jackson	South Carolina	1767–1845	1829–1837	Democrat	widower
Martin Van Buren	New York	1782–1862	1837–1841	Democrat	widower
William Henry Harrison	Virginia	1773–1841	1841	Whig	Anna Tuthill Symmes Harrison
John Tyler	Virginia	1790–1862	1841–1845	Whig	Letitia Christian Tyler Julia Gardiner Tyler
James Polk	North Carolina	1795–1849	1845–1849	Democrat	Sarah Childress Polk

Our PRESIDENTS

President	Birthplace	Life Dates	Term	Political Party	First Lady
Zachary Taylor	Virginia	1784–1850	1849–1850	Whig	Margaret Mackall Smith Taylor
Millard Fillmore	New York	1800–1874	1850–1853	Whig	Abigail Powers Fillmore
Franklin Pierce	New Hampshire	1804–1869	1853–1857	Democrat	Jane Means Appleton Pierce
James Buchanan	Pennsylvania	1791–1868	1857–1861	Democrat	never married
Abraham Lincoln	Kentucky	1809–1865	1861–1865	Republican	Mary Todd Lincoln
Andrew Johnson	North Carolina	1808–1875	1865–1869	Democrat	Eliza McCardle Johnson
Ulysses S. Grant	Ohio	1822–1885	1869–1877	Republican	Julia Dent Grant
Rutherford B. Hayes	Ohio	1822–1893	1877–1881	Republican	Lucy Ware Webb Hayes
James A. Garfield	Ohio	1831–1881	1881	Republican	Lucretia Rudolph Garfield
Chester A. Arthur	Vermont	1829–1886	1881–1885	Republican	widower
Grover Cleveland	New Jersey	1837–1908	1885–1889	Democrat	Frances Folsom Cleveland

Our PRESIDENTS

President	Birthplace	Life Dates	Term	Political Party	First Lady
Benjamin Harrison	Ohio	1833–1901	1889–1893	Republican	Caroline Lavina Scott Harrison
Grover Cleveland	New Jersey	1837–1908	1893–1897	Democrat	Frances Folsom Cleveland
William McKinley	Ohio	1843–1901	1897–1901	Republican	Ida Saxton McKinley
Theodore Roosevelt	New York	1858–1919	1901–1909	Republican	Edith Kermit Carow Roosevelt
William Howard Taft	Ohio	1857–1930	1909–1913	Republican	Helen Herron Taft
Woodrow Wilson	Virginia	1856–1924	1913–1921	Democrat	Ellen L. Axson Wilson Edith Bolling Galt Wilson
Warren G. Harding	Ohio	1865–1923	1921–1923	Republican	Florence Kling De Wolfe Harding
Calvin Coolidge	Vermont	1872–1933	1923–1929	Republican	Grace Anna Goodhue Coolidge
Herbert Hoover	Iowa	1874–1964	1929–1933	Republican	Lou Henry Hoover
Franklin D. Roosevelt	New York	1882–1945	1933–1945	Democrat	Anna Eleanor Roosevelt Roosevelt
Harry S. Truman	Missouri	1884–1972	1945–1953	Democrat	Elizabeth "Bess" Virginia Wallace Truman

Our PRESIDENTS

President	Birthplace	Life Dates	Term	Political Party	First Lady
Dwight D. Eisenhower	Texas	1890–1969	1953–1961	Republican	Mamie Geneva Doud Eisenhower
John F. Kennedy	Massachusetts	1917–1963	1961–1963	Democrat	Jacqueline Lee Bouvier Kennedy
Lyndon Baines Johnson	Texas	1908–1973	1963–1969	Democrat	Claudia "Lady Bird" Alta Taylor Johnson
Richard M. Nixon	California	1913–1994	1969–1974	Republican	Thelma "Pat" Catherine Patricia Ryan Nixon
Gerald R. Ford	Nebraska	1913–	1974–1977	Republican	Elizabeth "Betty" Bloomer Warren Ford
James Earl Carter	Georgia	1924–	1977–1981	Democrat	Rosalynn Smith Carter
Ronald Reagan	Illinois	1911–2004	1981–1989	Republican	Nancy Davis Reagan
George Bush	Massachusetts	1924–	1989–1993	Republican	Barbara Pierce Bush
William J. Clinton	Arkansas	1946–	1993–2001	Democrat	Hillary Rodham Clinton
George W. Bush	Connecticut	1946–	2001–	Republican	Laura Welch Bush

Presidential FACTS

Qualifications
To run for president, a candidate must
- be at least 35 years old
- be a citizen who was born in the United States
- have lived in the United States for 14 years

Term of Office
A president's term of office is four years. No president can stay in office for more than two terms.

Election Date
The presidential election takes place every four years on the first Tuesday of November.

Inauguration Date
Presidents are inaugurated on January 20.

Oath of Office
I do solemnly swear I will faithfully execute the office of the President of the United States and will to the best of my ability preserve, protect, and defend the Constitution of the United States.

Write a Letter to the President
One of the best things about being a U.S. citizen is that Americans get to participate in their government. They can speak out if they feel government leaders aren't doing their jobs. They can also praise leaders who are going the extra mile. Do you have something you'd like the president to do? Should the president worry more about the environment and encourage people to recycle? Should the government spend more money on our schools? You can write a letter to the president to say how you feel!

1600 Pennsylvania Avenue
Washington, D.C. 20500

You can even send an e-mail to: president@whitehouse.gov

For Further INFORMATION

Internet Sites

Learn more about President Wilson:
http://www.americanpresident.org/KoTrain/Courses/WW/WW_In_Brief.htm

Read President Wilson's Fourteen Points speech to Congress:
http://www.lib.byu.edu/~rdh/wwi/1918/14points.html

Visit Wilson's birthplace:
http://www.woodrowwilson.org/index2.html

Visit the Wilsons' House in Washington, D.C., where he lived after the presidency:
http://www.woodrowwilsonhouse.org

Read President Wilson's speech asking Congress to declare war:
http://www.lib.byu.edu/~rdh/wwi/1917/wilswarm.html

Learn more about World War I:
http://www.thecorner.org/wwi/wwi.htm

Learn more about the Nobel Peace Prize:
http://www.nobel.se/peace/index.html

Learn more about all the presidents and visit the White House:
http://www.whitehouse.gov/WH/glimps/presidents/html/presidents/html
http://www.thepresidency.org/presinfo.htm
http://www.american presidents.org/

Books

Mead, Gary. *The Doughboys: America and the First World War.* New York: Overlook Press, 2000.

Rogers, James T. *Woodrow Wilson: Visionary for Peace.* New York: Facts on File, 1997.

Stein, R. Conrad. *The United Nations* (Cornerstones of Freedom). Chicago: Childrens Press, 1994.

Index